To Jacque
I adore you!
You will rock at
coaching!
Deb

WORDABULOUS!

Celebrating the '**Positive Power**' of Words

By Debbie Watts

National Vocabulary Championship Coach of the Year

Shine Time Books

Wordabulous!
Celebrating the 'Positive Power' of Words

Shine Time Books
P.O. Box 331941
Nashville, TN 37203

© 2009 By Debbie Watts

All rights reserved, including the right of reproduction in whole or in part in any form.

Shine Time Books is a division of Whiting Publicity & Promotions

For information about special discounts for bulk purchases, please call toll-free
at 1-888-80-SHINE; send an e-mail to Info@Shinetime.com;
or visit www.ShineTimeBooks.com.

Cover art and book layout by Brian T. Cox
Author photograph by Dan Loftin
Publicity by Chuck Whiting

Manufactured in the United States of America

10 9 8 7 6 5 4 3 2

Library of Congress Control Number: 2009923581

ISBN: 978-0-9712398-90

This is the third book by award-winning author Debbie Watts. Her other
books are *Eat My Chalk Dust: Creative Teaching With a Sense of Humor* and
Diary of a Nashville Lady: Recollection & Recipes. Shine Time Books also has
published the holiday book and music CD, *The Littlest Star: a musical story.*

ACKNOWLEDGEMENTS

To: My students, who have taught me much more than I could ever teach them.

To: David Nurnberg of Civic Entertainment Group in New York, who encouraged me in the creation of my persona, 'Word Woman'.

To: Mike Bevan and the Game Show Network for creating the National Vocabulary Championship, and for giving me the award as National Coach of the Year.

To: The county education official who suggested that I take a writing class.

To: My publisher and publicist, Chuck Whiting, for believing in me.

Fore-Words

For as long as I can remember, I have loved words. A talkative and literate child, at an early age I discovered that everything that mattered to me could be obtained or retained by the correct usage of the right words. Though I didn't always use them at the right time, I knew that there was undeniable power in words. It was inevitable that I would drift toward careers in which words would play a major role. And so it was that I became a teacher, a writer, a television producer, (indulge me here) a guru of grammar, a high priestess of pronouns and prepositions, a comma-mama, and, among other things, a woman of words, i.e. "Word Woman".

With 20 years of experience as a television writer, producer, and performer in my background, and with two small children to raise as a single parent, I made the decision to return to teaching. When I did, I quickly learned how similar a day at school was to a day in the television studio. Each presentation was a potential production, and that students came to expect nothing less of me than that each lesson have a theatrical flair. Thus, as I reviewed the parts of speech with a class of sixth graders, it was natural that we create a series of song parodies, such as "Charlie Brown" by the Coasters becoming a song about prepositions, featuring the immortal line: "Over, under, in and out. That's what prepositions are about."

When I wanted to be sure that my sixth grade would remember that we reviewed the rules for comma usage, together we created a rap about comma rules, and in my teacher-rapper persona, I became "Comma Mama", complete with dark glasses and gangsta gold.

Finally, when I was asked to coach our high school students to participate in the national vocabulary championship, a competition whose prize was over $40,000 in college scholarships, my persona became "Word Woman", a superhero unabashedly modeled after television superhero, "Wonder Woman". Complete with boomerang tiara, wrist deflectors, and word bank, my character daily fought a teacher's arch-enemy, apathy. I rewarded deposits into the word bank, i.e. collections of "new words" on index cards, with extra points. As we shared the new words in class, I observed their interest in the fact that there were many words they didn't know. As I coached the delegates to the championship finals, a televised game show, I used the materials and modules generated by the Princeton Review. I could see that in the lives of high school students, there were always new words to learn. I was validated when one of them would come to me and share that he had used that word in conversation, or in a written report, or letter to a university. When I was notified that I had been selected National Vocabulary Championship Coach of the Year for my efforts as "Word Woman", I was not only gratified that my attention-getting behavior must've yielded some results, but that perhaps people of all ages and careers could benefit from what I call "adventures in vocabulary".

Thus, the concept "wordabulous" was born. It embraces the fact that no matter how old a person is, no matter how much education he has, no matter what job he does, his life can be improved, enjoyed, and, if you will, celebrated, through the knowledge and appreciation of words. Even President Obama could benefit from one of my specialized "word-makeovers". In the following pages, I share some thoughts about words, some "words of wisdom", and some chapters arranged in a "word-a-week" configuration. The examples I have chosen to use are strictly my own preference. There is a larger world of words out there, and the reader is encouraged to "find his own" vocabulary that will serve him best, let him grow, and, in short, "be wordabulous".

I sincerely hope that the reader will enjoy the sense of humor I occasionally inject. I believe that many, at least in my generation, have become "turned off" by stuffy grammarians. I'm a firm believer that we all need not to take ourselves too seriously, and, as for me and my house, we will live largely, love generously, and speak and write "wordabulously".

Contents

'Wordabulous' Defined	1
'Words, Words, Words'. . . of Wisdom	2
Thoughts and Tips	8
Words To Shape the 21st Century	11
Buzzwords	16
I Pheme, You Pheme, Euphemes	21
Teenspeak and Text Message Lingo	24
'You Don't Say'	26
Commonly Misspelled Words	29
Commonly Misused Words	34
My Favorite Words	39
Spinning Latin	43
Thanks To The Bard	46
BYOW (Bring Your Own Words)	49
Say the Word – The Role Games Play	51
Wordabulous Classroom Activities	58

'WORDABULOUS' DEFINED

What is "Wordabulous"? It's a philosophy, a positive outlook, and a lifestyle. Philosophically speaking, it's the belief that anyone and everyone can have a better life, a more stimulating life, a more outreaching life, through the power of words. Words are the under-rated low-hanging fruit of the 21st Century, and they're waiting there for everyone, in the pages of a dictionary, in a great book, in a thought-provoking lecture, in the next conversation. Words have the power to transform; if they are positive, they can uplift the hopeless, challenge the erudite, and entertain the jaded. Those who master the art of positive words may ultimately "rule the world", or at least their immediate vicinity. They can also inspire and encourage, and by being lifelong learners themselves, can adopt a childlike wonder about everything around them. Accompanying that childlike wonder is an exhilaration that using the right word at the right time can precipitate. It's living large, loving life, and learning to love. . . the unpretentious beauty of . . . words.

Anyone can live wordabulous-ly. Through the pages of this book, hopefully, "wordabulous" can describe you!

'WORDS, WORDS, WORDS' OF WISDOM

Words, words, words. – Hamlet by William Shakespeare

In the beginning was the Word, and the Word was with God, and the Word was God. – John 1:1

A word fitly spoken is like apples of gold in pictures of silver. – Proverbs 25:11

An honest man's word is as good as his bond. – Miguel de Cervantes

A little word in kindness spoken,
A motion or a tear,
Has often healed the heart that's broken,
And made a friend sincere. – A Little Word

A word is dead
When it is said,
Some say.
I say it just
Begins to live
That day. – Emily Dickinson

Music is love in search of a word. – Sidney Lanier

. . . insist upon having the meaning of a word clearly understood before using it. – John Stuart Mill

Man's word is God in man. – Alfred, Lord Tennyson

How long a time lies in one little word. – William Shakespeare

It is not of so much consequence what you say, as how you say it. Memorable sentences are memorable on account of some single irradiating word. – Alexander Smith

There is a weird power in a spoken word. . . And a word carries far – very far – deals destruction through time as the bullets go flying through space. – Joseph Conrad

Whatever kind of word thou speakest the like shalt thou hear. – GREEK ANTHOLOGY

The word-coining genius, as if thought plunged into a sea of words and came up dripping. – Virginia Woolf, about Shakespeare

Words are the daughters of earth, and things are the sons of heaven. – Samuel Johnson

Words are like leaves; and where they most abound, much fruit of sense beneath is rarely found. – Alexander Pope

Words are the physicians of a mind diseased. – Heraclitus

Words are women; deeds are men. – George Herbert

In words, as fashions, the same rule will hold
Alike fantastic of too new or old.
Be not the first by whom new are tried,
Nor yet the last to lay the old aside. – Alexander Pope

It hurleth not the tongue to give fair words. – John Heywood

God wove a web of loveliness,
Of coulds and stars and birds,
But made not anything of all
So beautiful as words. – Anna Branch

Poetry teaches the enormous force of a few words, and, in proportion to the inspiration, checks loquacity. – Parnassus

Good words are worth much, and cost little. – George Herbert

Words ought to be a little wild for they are the assault of thoughts on the unthinking. – John Maynard Keynes

Men of few words are the best men. – William Shakespeare

Bright is the ring of words when the right man rings them. – Robert Louis Stevenson

A word, once sent abroad, flies irrevocably. – Horace

Learn the right of coining words in the quick mint of joy. – Leigh Hunt

Words are easy, like the wind. – Richard Barnfield

. . . it is often the happy fortune of the aphorist to drag from its obscurity some such dim intuition, or confused bit of experience, to clothe it in words, and bring it into daylight for our delighted recognition. – Logan Pearsall Smith

Once a word has been allowed to escape, it cannot be recalled. – Rudyard Kipling

A word is not a crystal, transparent, unchanged; it is the skin of a living thought and may vary greatly in color and content according to the circumstances and the time in which it is used.
– Oliver Wendell Holmes

Words are, of course, the most powerful drug used by mankind.
– Rudyard Kipling

Do not the most moving moments of our lives find us all without words? – Marcell Marceau

I love smooth words, like gold-enameled fish. – Elinor Wylie, *Pretty Words*

It is the man who determines what is said, not the words. – Henry David Thoreau

Colors fade, temples crumble, empires fall, but wise words endure.
– Edward Thorndike

Kind words can be short and easy to speak, but their echoes are truly endless. – Mother Teresa

If you would be pungent, be brief, for it is with words as with sunbeams - - the more they are condensed, the deeper they burn.
– Robert Southey

A fool and his words are soon parted. – William Shakespeare

Words are weapons, and it is dangerous to borrow them from the arsenal of the enemy. – George Santayana

Words sing. They hurt. They teach. They sanctify. They were man's first, immeasurable feat of magic. They liberated us from ignorance and our barbarous past. – Leo Calvin Rosten

Words must surely be counted among the most powerful drugs man ever invented. – Leo Calvin Rosten

Abuse of words has been the great instrument of sophistry and chicanery of party, faction, and division of society. – John Adams

A synonym is a word you use when you can't spell the word you first thought of. – Burt Bacharach

A word is a bud attempting to become a twig. How can one not dream while writing? It is the pen which dreams. The blank page gives the right to dream. – Gaston Bachelard

You can taste a word. – Pearl Bailey

For your born writer, nothing is so healing as the realization that he has come upon the right word. – Catherine Drinker Bowen

A blow with a word strikes deeper than a blow with a sword.
– Robert Burton

Short words are best and the old words when short are best of all.
– Winston Churchill

Some of mankind's most terrible misdeeds have been committed under the spell of certain magic words or phrases. – James Bryant Conant

The basic tool for the manipulation of reality is the manipulation of words. If you can control the meaning of words, you can control the people who use the words. – Philip K. Dick

Every word was once a poem. – Ralph Waldo Emerson

When ideas fail, words come in very handy. – Johann Wolfgang von Goethe

THOUGHTS AND TIPS FROM 'WORD WOMAN'

I don't claim to be an expert on words – only one who loves and respects them. Here are some of my own thoughts about words and tips for increasing one's vocabulary:

Thomas Jefferson said that he couldn't live without books.
I can't live without words.

There's a world in a word.
The last word in "Sword" is "word". Think about it.
Make your words sweet. You may be eating them later.
A kind word can calm an angry tidal wave.
Some people are worldly. I want to be "wordly".
Words are like dolls. You can dress them up and play with them.
It's a 'syn' not to use a Thesaurus. It's filled with 'syn'onyms.

Want a better vocabulary?
Read. Read more.
Write. Write more.
Use a dictionary.
Use a Thesaurus.
Occasionally, write a letter instead of an e-mail.
Occasionally, turn off the television and discuss a book.
Read a book together.
Go out into an open space and read a book – aloud.
Play Scrabble, Password, hangman and work crossword puzzles.
Watch television game shows that are word games.
Read Shakespeare. It's not as difficult as you may think.
Read poetry aloud.

Write poetry.
Take part in seminar discussions.
Join a book club.
Read children's books to a child.
Listen more than you speak.
Keep a "new word" journal.
Read book reviews.
Write a book review.
Write your autobiography.
Write a letter to a congressman.
Let someone proofread something you have written.
Go to lectures.
Read the Bible. It's still the greatest book ever written.

Learn to love words. They are your friends.

WORDS TO SHAPE THE 21ST CENTURY

Like it or not, we are in the space age, the high-tech age, and the business age. Communication is advancing by leaps and bounds, and the less-than-savvy person could get left behind. The words in this chapter are arranged like an A-B-C book for adults. If you already use these words, you should feel comfortable that these words can help you navigate the communication gauntlet. If you learn a new word or two in the following set, your purchase will be worth it. I hope you enjoy my commentary. Try to use one of the following each week:

Analog – Not to be confused with the way that some seventh graders like to define a preposition. . . "anything a frog can do to a log. . ." Analog is continuous transmission of information to our senses.

Attached – From the entertainment industry, this term denotes that an actor has interest in a project, so as to interest a studio or group of investors.

Blackberry – It's not just for muffins anymore. If you don't know about this communication device, you may be seriously behind in the world of high-tech communication.

Blog – Not to be confused with the classic horror film, *The Blob*, this term is short for weblog. A list of journal entries posted on a web page.

Cookie – Not just for breakfast anymore, it's data sent to your computer by a web server that records your actions on a certain web site.

Coterie – A group of people who associate closely.

Del.icio.us – A community bookmarking web site where users may share. Not being naturally technological, computer-speak is not my idea of the traditional definition of delicious, but it does make me wonder why so many computer terms seem to be derived from some of the joys of food.

Download – The process by which data is sent to one's computer. Not to be confused with down-low, a rapper-ish term for keeping hush-hush.

Excel – A spreadsheet program for Windows. Personally, it has not allowed me to excel. . . not yet, that is.

Facebook – A social networking web site. Very popular with the high school set.

Flatbed – Back where I come from, this term meant that a boyfriend could actually pick you up for a date. It now refers to a scanner or copier that uses a flat, glass surface for scanning documents.

Global – Having to do with world-wide concerns, as in "Gasoline prices may have an effect on the global economy."

Green – Referring to being in harmony with the ecology. Famous muppet, Kermit the Frog, had a hit song that carried the sentiment, "It's not easy being green." How prophetic.

Hacker – In writer's jargon, it's one who "sells out", or writes schlock that will deliver a paycheck, rather than for literary edification. In recent years, it has come to mean one who can gain unauthorized access to other computers.

Hybrid – Formerly a horticultural term, now an automotive one.

Immersion – Again, where I come from, it's a method of baptism. In the 21st Century, it has come to mean becoming super-involved, especially when referring to video games.

iPod – If you don't already know this term, you must not be raising a middle schooler. It's a portable music player.

JPEG – Not to be confused with J-Lo, it's a compressed image file format. (Yawn)

Joystick – I won't even annotate here. It controls video games.

Kickback – A portion of income given as payment for having made the income possible.

Kiosk – If you haven't checked yourself in at the airport, where've you been?

Lingo – The jargon of a particular field.

Login – Your username and password to get into your computer.

Morph – As a verb, to change into a different form. As a noun, the changed form.

Mnemonic – A pattern that can be used as an aid for memorizing information. Later in the book, I'll offer some mnemonic spelling strategies.

Nosh – To snack, to munch, to lunch – with business associates. A means of networking

Nybble – Half a byte. Byte: a set of eight bits that represent a single character in the computer's memory. Note to self: Write another book on the "eating" vocabulary of computer science.

Oprah – A word expressing the "be-all and end-all".

Phishing – Attempting to steal personal information.

Piano – Okay, I said these words were personal. It's how I spell relief from computer stress. It (the playing of it) is one of the few remaining skills that involve a human being. Oh, I know that you can buy the pre-programmed discs, but, after all, can they take requests? ? ? ? Perhaps this is one job I'll always have.

Queue – Pronounced like the letter "Q". A list of jobs waiting to be processed, and a good word in a game of Scrabble.

Qwerty – Term used to describe a standard keyboard. It gets its name from the first six keys in the upper left row of the keyboard.

Re-invention – See Madonna.

Ruby – Object-oriented programming language.

Server – "My name is Earthlink, and I'll be your server today." It serves info to computers that link to it.

Synergy – A phenomenon in which two or more discrete influences or agents acting together create an effect greater than that predicted by knowing the separate effects of the individuals.

Texting – Text messaging. Has its own lingo. And its own chapter later in this book.

Trojan Horse – In Greek mythology, it was a crafty war strategy. In the world of computers, it's a software program that can masquerade as a regular program.

Ubiquitous – Being everywhere. One of my favorite Latin derivatives.

URL – Uniform Resource Locator. Now, aren't you glad you bought this book?

Virtual Reality – Illusion of reality created by a computer system. It's also where we may be headed in television.

Wi-Fi – Short for wireless fidelity.

Wi-ki – From the Hawaiian phrase, "wiki wiki", which means very very fast, it's a web site that allows users to add and update content on the site using their own web browser.

Xerox – A brand name for a copy machine. As the term "Kleenex" is used to mean "tissue", this term, as a verb, means "to copy".

X – Thank the Lord, mine is out of state.

Yahoo – One definition is an "uncultivated person". It's also the largest web portal.

Youthspeak – The language of texting.

Zetabyte – Again, not to be confused with actress Zeta-Jones. It's one sextillion bytes. If one consumes all those "bytes", could "zeta-lypo" be far behind? ? ? ? ? ? ?

Zip – A compressed file.

BUZZWORDS

The term "buzzword" is in itself a buzzword. Wikipedia defines it as "a vague idiom whose cloudy meaning can impress one's audience with a pretense of knowledge." Whether or not you perceive the term "buzzword" as a negative, or cliché, the fact is that even if you make a conscious effort not to use buzzwords, you will hear them used by others. If nothing else, a quick handbook glossary can let you know if the user is a schmoozer, i.e. someone who is using words to hide a lack of knowledge or understanding of what he is talking about. What constitutes a "buzzword" to you (words you personally encounter to excess) may be a legitimate new word to someone else. Again, I arrange these in A-B-C, word-a-week style. I have chosen words from business, technology, ecology and communication media. Some are "valid" terminology whose usage is to communicate effectively and concisely. Others may be over-used and "used-to-confuse". At any rate, know what they mean, and you have power. As you encounter others, make your own list. Hope you enjoy my asides, as these are strictly personal.

Agenda – A list of things to be done. Often has a negative connotation, as when referring to a "hidden" one of these.

At the end of the day – This one is beginning to grate on me. Means ultimately.

Blamestorming – Talk session after a major project, during which time co-workers get personal about what worked and what didn't.

Broad strokes – An outline. Sounds like a good title for a sitcom about three ladies who operate a massage parlor.

Chips and salsa – Hard and software.

Clickthrough – A way of measuring success of an on-line ad company.

Dilberted – Named for the comic-book character, to be "Dilberted" means to be oppressed by the boss.

Downsizing – Laying off.

Empower – To increase individual strength by developing self-confidence.

Exit strategy – Means of escaping one's current situation. Paul Simon came up with a series of these in a clever song, one of whose lines said, "Drop off the key, Lee."

Facilitate – To make easy.

Focused – As an adjective, such as "client-focused".

Go ahead – I need you to "go ahead. . ." and do whatever I want you to do.

Golden parachute – Perks added to "facilitate" an "exit strategy".

Heads up – To give helpful, preliminary information.

Helicopter – One who hovers obtrusively.

Impact – As a verb, "to have an effect on".

Issues – Aren't we all tired of hearing. . . "I have issues with . . ." meaning matters in dispute.

Jargoning – The act of using industry buzzwords.

Jump the Shark – A defining moment at which an entity (in the entertainment industry, such as a long-running television series) goes past its peak of interest.

Knowledge transfer – An exchange of info.

Kool Aid – As in "drink the. . . " means to stop protesting, deny one's own will, and do what the boss tells you to do.

Leverage – Power to act effectively or to influence people.

Low-hanging fruit – A business opportunity which can be obtained easily.

Mindshare – A company's ability to retain a piece of the public's consciousness.

Multi-tasking – It sounded so cool at first; now it's a way of life for most of us.

Nimby – Began as an acronym, NIMBY, meaning "not in my back yard", to refer to opposition of something objectionable.

Nugget(ing) – As a verb, it means to "look for the gems" within a long speech or memo.

On the runway – An off-the-record conversation.

On the same page – Two entities who generally agree or have the same beliefs.

Pro-active – To prevent, or to "facilitate" before the fact. Has acquired somewhat of a nasty connotation in the business world.

Push the envelope – Test a policy to the extremes.

Quirky – Peculiar, as in a personality.

Quietus – To stop.

Raise the bar – To challenge by surpassing expectations.

Run it up the flagpole – Test market.

Sea change – From Shakespeare's *The Tempest*. Power shift at the office.

Sitcoms – Single-income. One parent stays home with two kids. Oppressive mortgage.

Texting – Text messaging. I know. It's on the other list, too. It's a giant.

Thinking outside the Box – I'm not sure that the first person ever to use this phrase really knew what he was talking about. It sounded cool for awhile. Now, like multi-tasking, it's a way of life for many.

Unplugged – Disconnected from anything hi-tech. An "unplugged" conversation is one that is between two human beings.

Updated – Time management strategies.

Value added – Like texting and multi-tasking, in the beginning it was a respectable notion to provide more "bang for your buck". (another buzzword)

Virtual – In cyberspace. On the computer. Simulation.

Watercooler – A euphemism for office gossip.

Wellness – Balance between mind and body.

X (Generation X, that is) – Those recent college grads who don't know where they're going or what they want.

Xerox Subsidy – Swiping free copies from the office.

Y'all – You all.

Youth Market – That which appeals to generation X.

Zero – As in "zero tolerance".

Zero-coupon bond – A bond bought at a price lower than its face value.

I PHEME, YOU PHEME, EUPHEMES

You may use these types of expressions daily and not know what they're called. When you "talk around" something so as to "clean it up", or make it less blunt or offensive, you may use a euphemism. The word "eupheme" comes from the Greek eu (good) and pheme (speech). Thus, a eupheme, or euphemism means auspicious or good word or speech. The most common usage of a euphemism is to make a concept less offensive and more acceptable. The term "spin doctor" is in itself a euphemism; it's a professional whose job it is to use language to control damage or change or soften public opinion. Since in the 21st Century we are all called upon to be public relations experts to a certain extent, we unconsciously "spin" to make a statement more palatable, or politically correct.

In some cases, euphemisms evade the truth, and it is as much our job to make inferences in the speeches of others so as to translate the true meaning as well as it is our job to make statements more acceptable ourselves. The following is not a complete list by any means. I've classified euphemisms into the following categories: corporemisms (used by corporate America), edu-speak (used by educators), minced oaths, sexemisms, and eubodisms (used to "clean up" bodily functions). Then, there's a category of miscellaneous, many of which we've heard and used.

Corporemisms (which include business, military and political)

Euphemism	Literal meaning
Involuntary force reductions	Lay-offs
Focussed reductions	" "
Streamlining	" "
Reshaping	" "
Pink-slipped	Terminated, Fired
Canned	" "
Let go	" "

Visually impaired	Blind
Sightless	" "
"To spend more time with my family"	I quit
Friendly fire	Accidentally killed by your own side
Neutralizing the target	Killing the enemy on purpose
Collateral damage	Killing the enemy by mistake
Pro-life	Anti-abortion
Contributions	Tax increases
Physically challenged	Handicapped
Gender	Sex
Diversity; ethnicity	Race
Sub-optimal	Failed
Temporarily displaced inventory	Stolen goods
Synthetic glass	Plastic

Edu-speak

Low motivation	Lazy
Aggressive	Bully
Imaginative	Lies
Distracted	Not doing his work
Challenged	Incapable

Minced Oaths:

Darn it	Dammit
Dagnabbit	" "
Dadgummit	" "
Gosh, golly	God
Gee	Jesus

Sexual:

Baseball metaphors, first base, etc.	Degrees of sexual advances
Score	Sexual conquest
The pill	Oral contraceptive
Love glove, party hat, diving suit	Condom
Gay, light in the loafers, straight as a circle	Homosexual male
Dyke, bulldyke, butch	Homosexual female

Bodily functions

"Powder my nose"	Find a ladies' restroom
"See a man about a dog"	Find a men's restroom
Pee, do-do, poo-poo	Baby language for elimination
Number one, number two	Emptying bladder, bowel

Sometimes, we use letter abbreviations:
SOB, GD, BS, PDQ, BFD

Abstractions:
Going to the other side, pass away, buy the farm, kick the bucket.

Indirections:
Behind, bottom, unmentionables, privates, go to the bathroom.

Understatements:
"Not exactly thin", "not bright".

There's an entire slate of euphemisms for low intelligence:
A couple of sandwiches shy of a picnic
A couple of fries short of a happy meal
Not the sharpest knife in the drawer
His butter slid off his biscuit
Elevator doesn't go all the way up
No grain in the silo

Her brains fell on her	Large-busted and stupid

This list does not include all the euphemisms ever uttered. This segment was meant to inform the reader that everyone "cleans up a phrase", and that these phrases are called euphemisms.

TEENSPEAK AND TEXT MESSAGE LINGO

Text message lingo is its own language. In order to fit an entire message on a screen, this abbrev-speak has evolved. Whether you agree with many teachers who feel that text-speak is at least partly to blame for students' reluctance to write a complete paragraph, or a complete sentence for that matter, or if you are an extremist who believes that subverting our youth is a terrorist plot to attack from extremely within, the fact is, text messaging is here. It's a form of communication. Cover the right hand side of the page as you look at the left-hand column. See how many you can decipher. Again, this is not a complete list. It's a one-a-week addition to your vocabulary. Let the youth of America contribute to your becoming wordabulous.

AAYF	As always, your friend
ADIP	Another day in paradise
BB	Be back
BFF	Best friends forever
CB	Chat-brat, or coffee break
CF	Coffee Freak
Debbie (I had to include this one)	Newer than a newbie
DKDC	Don't know, don't care
EOM	End of Message
EZ	Easy
F	Sorry. . . I couldn't find a clean one.
GAL	Get a Life
GL	Good luck, or get lost
HB	Hurry back
HHIS	Hanging head in shame
IBK	Idiot behind keyboard
ICQ	I seek you
JFI	Just for information (it's the new FYI)
JOOTT	Just one of those things
KBD	Keyboard
KOTL	Kiss On The Lips

LFTI	Looking forward to it
LOL	Laughing out loud, or lots of love
MHOTY	My hat's off to you
MYL	Mind your language (I'm glad to see this one)
NAVY	Never again volunteer yourself
NIMBY	Not in my back yard
OBO	Or best offer
OMDB	Over my dead body
P&C	Private and confidential
PHAT	Pretty hot and tempting
QLS	Reply
QQ	Quick question
RBTL	Read between the lines
SHB	Should have been
SITD	Still in the dark
TAH	Take a hike
TCB	Trouble came back
U2	You, too
U8	You ate?
VBG	Very big grin
VWD	Very well done
WDDD	Whoopie Doo Da Dey
WE	Whatever
XME	Excuse me
XOXO	Hugs and Kisses
YGBK	You gotta be kidding
YOYO	You're on your own
ZIP	Data compression technology
ZZZ	Sleeping, bored

YOU DON'T SAY. . . . .#*&!

There is nothing inherently wrong with any word in any language, nor is there anything inherently wrong with the sound of a word. It's the connotation of that word, the image the word brings to mind. Different words mean different things to different people. What is offensive to me may not be offensive to the next person. However, this is my book, so I have identified some words that make me feel uncomfortable.

Perhaps, in my case, it goes all the way back to my teen years when I was traumatized by an athletic coach's constant swearing. There are still some words that make me cringe to this day. There are different schools of thought on why people swear, curse, take the name of the Lord in vain, whatever you want to call it. There is a variety of interesting books and articles on the subject of why people curse. In the book *Why We Curse,* Timothy Jay concludes that two-thirds of the time, people resort to a limited vocabulary when they are angry. Some people, on the other hand, seem to believe that, if they sprinkle curse words, it makes them sound more authoritative and passionate in their beliefs. I personally believe it's a matter of insecurity in themselves, and they feel that they will get attention if they swear.

Donna Jo Napoli, a professor of linguistics at Swarthmore College, believes that young people, in particular, have come to use curse words in a friendly, passé way, and they are not using aggression or trying to be offensive. I've experienced this thinking myself, having taught grades six through 12 for 20 years, and I will go so far as to say that from the time I began my teaching career until now, this de-sensitization has escalated 100 percent. Let's face it. The television and movies we watch, the video games we play, and the music we listen to have all become more and more profane. Now, I know I'm getting old. I sound like my own parents did 30 years ago.

Last but not least, there's the group of people who, by day, are mild-mannered, sweet souls who would not offend for anything. Then, after the third or fourth drink, not only does their language become more "seasoned", the volume goes up as well. I suppose they are to be pitied, but I still find myself being offended by their careless and sloppy speech. I have witnessed this phenomenon during 20 years as a nightclub pianist.

The late comic genius George Carlin named "seven words you can't say on television". I have my own list of five words that seem to offend me personally. When I began my research for this chapter, I didn't expect to delve into the etymologies of these words, but I'm personally glad I did. It helps to understand how the words originated in the first place. Since I don't say these words, I will describe some of them, rather than write them out.

Damn

Damn doesn't offend me. Short for damnation, it doesn't always mean that a person or thing is being condemned. It is often an expression of amazement, even of approval. I remember the first time I heard Rhett Butler's famous quote at the end of the film, *Gone With The Wind*. I actually recall gasping when he uttered the now immortal: "Frankly, my dear, I don't give a damn."

When someone adds the name of the Deity to the beginning, it does offend me. I could quote Bible verses here, but this book is not intended to moralize or legislate beliefs. It's a book about words. I only mean to say what offends me personally. Television will bleep out the "G-word" at the beginning of that profanity, leaving the "damn" to be heard.
I feel the same way when people casually use the name of Jesus. Likewise when they use such expressions as "Jesus, Mary and Joseph", and "Jesus H. Christ".

The "It" Word

I'll call this one the "it" word. It's slang for excrement the noun, or to deficate, the verb. I'd never heard the "myth" of how this word came to be until I read the story of manure being cargo on a ship (as if any society would ship manure). The story goes that several ships actually exploded because the methane gas emanating from the cargo ignited when sailors entered these cargo holds carrying lanterns. Thus, from that point on, the letters "S.H.I.T." were stamped on crates carrying the material. The letters stood for "Ship High In Transit".

The actual etymology traces the word back to the Old English noun "scite" and the Middle Low German "schite", both meaning dung. To me, it is an unpleasant, nasty-sounding utterance, and when spat out, sounds aggressive and mean.

The "Uck" Words

These I'll call the "uck" words. The first, the "f" word, may have come from an acronym meaning "fornication under consent of king" or "for unlawful carnal knowledge". The second I have had to outlaw in my classroom. The expression, "That –ucks!" has become acceptable somehow, but not to me. Both of these sound nasty and disrespectful, but, again, that's just me personally.

The "N" Word

Last but not least is the "n" word. In my opinion, it's the ugliest word in the English language because it expresses disrespect toward a person. Wikipedia says that it's a derogatory word used to refer to dark-skinned people, and it's the English variant of Negro. Negro is also a Spanish and Portuguese word, and the French call it negre. Mark Twain used the "n" word in his *Adventures of Tom Sawyer* and *Huckleberry Finn*. It was more an attempt at dialectical usage than disrespect in those works. However, over the years, many have used it disrespectfully, and it has actually come to mean "one who is a slave", having little to do with race.

I hope this segment has not offended anyone, and if it did, I'll just have to quote the pop music artist, Fergie, and say, "Oh, snap."

COMMONLY MISSPELLED WORDS

Many may disagree with me on the importance of correct spelling. I've even heard teachers console parents who may be lamenting the fact that their children are not good spellers by saying, "There's always spell-checker." The point is, spell-checker is not always there to help. There will always be situations in which we are called on to "spell-on-the-spot", such as, filling out job applications, taking writing assessments, etc. The fact is, if we strive to learn to spell correctly, we will be paid off in our grammar being better, our vocabulary being stronger, our being more communicative, and enjoying it more. In any endeavor, confidence breeds confidence. If we perform better in a given arena, we feel more like performing again. The following one-a-week list has been compiled from 20 years of experience in the classroom and 10 years of experience heading up a television writing staff. Perhaps some of the mnemonics I offer will stick in your mind and contribute to your own wordabulosity.

Accommodate – two c's, two m's.

A lot – I've seen this written as "alot" for the past 30 years. It's actually two words. I tell my middle school students to avoid this construction in the first place. It's lazy. You may substitute much, many, abundantly, etc., but not "a bunch". That's as lazy as "a lot".

Brake – A device for slowing a vehicle.

Break – A pause, or a destructive action.

Congratulations – Not congradulations. I've seen this one misspelled on church, even school bulletins. It could be being confused with "graduation".

Conscious/Conscience – The former describes an awake condition; the latter is the moral voice within.

Definitely – I've seen this one misspelled so many times and so many different ways, I now look it up each time I write it. The root word is "finite".

Desert/Dessert – The former is an arid area. The latter is a sweet following a meal. Think of the "ss" in the middle of the word as representing "so sweet".

Escape – Not "ex"cape.

Et cetera – Not "ex" cetera. I've heard teachers misuse this one.

Fiery – Not "firey".

Forfeit – Not "forfit".

Graffiti – Two f's; one t.

Grammar – Please don't spell it "grammer".

Harass – One r; double s. I'll keep my mnemonic for this one to myself.

Hygiene – If you're buying vowels for this one, it's one i and two e's.

Incredible – Suffix is "ible". Rhymes with "nibble".

Irrelevant – Double the "r". The "ir" prefix means "not".

Journal – Not "jurnal".

Judgment – The dictionary says that either spelling, "judgment" or "judgement" is acceptable.

Kindergarten - Not "garden".

Klutz – Meaning a clumsy person, not spelled "kluts".

License – Not "lisence".

Lien – Legal right to hold another's property.

Mischievous – Many pronounce an extra syllable here. It's not "mis-chee-vee-us".

Mnemonic – Helpful tricks for spelling strategies. Silent "m" at the beginning.

Mortgage – Silent "t".

Naïve – Pronounced "ni – eeve". Note the three vowels.

Niece – "I before e".

Occurred – Two c's; two r's.

Outre – Pronounced "oo-tray". Has the same French root as our English word, "other". Means eccentric. Different to the point of being deviant.

Oxymoron – It's neither an ox nor a moron. Nor is it a "miracle detergent". It's a figure of speech that uses seeming contradictions, such as "cruel kindness". See, that's value added for a chapter on spelling.

Parallel – The two l's come first.

Persevere – Contains the word, "severe". Not "servere". Means to persist.

Queue – Pronounced like the letter "Q". Two u's; two e's.

Quixotic – Knowing the origin of the word helps with the spelling. Allusion to fictional character, Don Quixote. The "x" in Quixote is pronounced like an "h". In the adjective here, which means extravagantly chivalrous, the "x" is pronounced like an "x".

Recommend – One "c"; double "m".

Rhythm – I've seen this one misspelled a variety of ways. Remember that there are two h's. The first one is silent.

Separate – Spelled the same as a verb or adjective.

Sincerely – When my classes write business letters, the spelling of this word must be reviewed. The tricky part is the "cere".

Their/there/they're – Possessive pronoun, adverb of place, contraction for they are.

To/too/two – Preposition, adverb meaning extreme or also, and number.

Usage – Root word is "use". Drop the "e".

Utopia – An ideal place. Pronounced "You"-topia.

Vacuum – One of the few words in the English language with a double "u".

Villain – "A" before "i".

Weird – "E" before "i".

Wield – "I" before "e".

Xylem – Like "z".

Yacht – Silent "ch".

Yield – Like "wield".

Zealot – zel-lot.

Zoology – Three o's.

COMMONLY MISUSED WORDS

After 20 years of teaching and editing, the following is my list of personal pet peeves. It in no way covers the entire scope of grammar, but you may find something in the list that you or others you communicate with misuse from time to time. I can't resist the occasional asides. Think about one of these each week, or read it all in one sitting, and while you do, marvel at our marvel-ous, "wordabulous" language.

Accept /Except – The former, to receive approval . The latter, with the exclusion of.

Allusion/Illusion – A literary reference and a false impression of reality.

Bazaar/Bizarre – A marketplace, and unusual, strange.

Bibliography/Biography – A list of sources and a nonfictional account of another's life.

Capital/Capitol – Differing from the lowercase letter in function and height, and seat of government.

Council/Counsel – An assembly of persons convened for advice, and advice itself, or a lawyer.

Decree/Degree – A formal order, and any of a series of steps.

Dual/Duel – Of or noting two; a pre-arranged combat.

Elicit/Illicit – To draw out, or evoke; not legal.

Farther/Further – At a greater distance; to a greater extent, or in addition.

Foul/fowl – Offensive to the senses, or a collision, or out of bounds on a playing field; one of several feathered creatures.

Gild/Guild – To coat with gold; an organization of persons with related interests.

Heal/Heel – To make whole; a dishonorable person.

Hole/Whole – An opening; complete.

Isle/Aisle – An island; a walkway between two rows.

Its/It's – Possessive pronoun (no apostrophe); contraction for it is.

Jest/Jist – A joke; the main idea.

Jibe/Jive – To be in harmony; slang for meaningless talk.

Killed/kilt – Past tense of kill; pleated Tartan skirt.

Know/No – To understand or process; negatory. (I'm not kidding. I still see this error.)

Lie/Lay – This one's tricky. In present tense, lie is intransitive: "I lie down each day after lunch." Lay is transitive and requires a direct object: "Lay the books down, and come with me." The past tense of lie is lay: "I lay in the sun for an hour yesterday."

Lead/Led – A heavy metal; the past tense of lead.

Many/A lot – Choose the word "many" as an adjective. I have spoken on this already.

Much/Very – I have a problem with the construction: "It was very fun." Be more specific in your description, such as: "The day at the beach was exhilarating." Or: "The movie we saw was entertaining."

Neither/Nor – When using neither, follow with nor: "Neither your father nor I will give permission."

Not/Double Negative – Do not use two "n" (negative) words in the same sentence except for neither/nor: A line from a classic song says, "I can't get no satisfaction." This constitutes a double negative because can't is a contraction for cannot. "Not and no" are a double negative, but, after all, Mick Jagger had poetic license.

Of/'ve – Of should not be confused with 've, the contraction of have in such constructions as: "I should've (not should of) arrived on time for the meeting."

Ought – Use "ought to", not "shouldn't ought".

Preposition – Shows a relationship between two words. Examples: in, on, to, of. . . .

Pronoun antecedent – A pronoun must agree with its antecedent, or the noun which it refers to in the same sentence. I hear (or worse, see on public signs or inter-office e-mails), "Each student must bring their own book." Should be: "Each student must bring his or her book."

Quiet/Quite – The former is an adjective: "Please be quiet in the library." The latter is an adverb: "The lunch was quite filling."

Quote – Use quotation marks around a direct quote: "Please pass the salt," he said.

Raise/Rise – Like lay and lie. Raise is transitive, and takes a direct object: "Raise the flag." Rise is intransitive: "The bread will rise in the oven."

Right/Write – I've seen this error: "I don't like to right essays." Obviously. This is a careless error, made in haste. Proofread. Proofread.

Sea/See – One is a body of water. The other means to encounter visually.

Stationary/Stationery – Not movable; writing paper.

Threw/Through – Past tense of throw; a preposition.

Than/Then – The former, a conjunction: "No one was more surprised than I." The latter, an adverb: "What do we do, then?"

Un – A prefix meaning not.

Usage – General mechanics of grammar.

Vain/Vein – Self-centered; mineral deposit, or carrier of blood in the body.

Very – Don't overuse. Be more creative, precise.

Who/Whom – Who is subjective: "Who is going to the ball game?" Whom is objective, as in, direct and indirect object, or object of preposition: "To whom shall I direct the question?"

Who's/Whose – A contraction for who is; a possessive pronoun. Again, the possessive pronoun has no apostrophe.

Ex – A prefix meaning former.

Xerox – Proper noun. Capitalize.

Your/You're – A possessive pronoun. "Don't forget your rain coat." Contraction for you are: "You're the best candidate for the office."

Yoke/Yolk – A burden; egg yellow. Once I was asked to "watch" the grammar of a writer on a cooking show whose job was to write the recipes on a graphic. Constantly, I had to correct this error: "Two egg yokes".

Z's – When forming the plural of an alphabet letter, use apostrophe and s.

Zen – Buddhist movement. Capitalized.

MY FAVORITE WORDS

A song from *The Sound of Music* says, "These are a few of my favorite things." The following list includes a few of my favorite words. I have chosen them for their positive influence; consequently, this list could be called, "Words to get you what you want". That is not to say that they are manipulative in a bad way. They're just positive. And positivity yields "wordabulosity".

Ad infinitum – Without limits. This phrase derived from Latin expresses faith in what human beings can do.

Addendum – From Latin also. Don't worry. Not all of them will be. I just love the words Latin gave us. An addition, especially to a written document. Since I always have more to say, i.e., more to ask for, I use this addition frequently. I give much, and I expect much from others.

Bona fide – In good faith, without deception or fraud.

Bouyant – Cheerful.

Californi-awesome – My own coinage. Adjective to describe the progressive, upbeat, creative atmosphere of many things California, where there are many like me.

Debacle – A disaster or fiasco.

Deft – Skillful, nimble.

Eclectic – Composed of elements from various sources. See Californi-awesome.

Enigma – A puzzle, riddle or inexplicable situation.

Fabulous – Almost impossible to believe. Blended with "word" to make the word, "Wordabulous".

Finesse – Delicacy or subtlety of persona or skill.

Gregarious – Fond of the company of others.

Gumption – Initiative.

Harbinger – One who heralds the advent of something.

Herculean – Requiring extraordinary strength.

Idiosyncrasy – A habit or mannerism peculiar to an individual.

Ironic – Having characteristics of irony, or the use of words to convey a meaning that is the opposite of its literal meaning.

Jaunty – Easy and sprightly in manner or bearing.

Jettison – A verb meaning to cast aside. Though it has its origin in sailing jargon, it has come to be used in referring to discarding a plan or strategy.

Kibitz – To criticize, heckle.

Kudos – Honor, proper respect.

Lickety-split – At great speed.

Linguosity – A Word-Woman coinage. Noun which names facility with the language.

Melifluous – Sweetly flowing, as a well-written speech.

Montage – Combination of pictorial or other elements into a single composition.

Niche – Place or position.

Nosh - Power snacking. We must keep up our strength.

Obligatory – Required.

Overt – Open to view, with no attempt to conceal.

Parlay – To bet on a subsequent contest.

Please – Never underestimate the power of this word.

Quid Pro Quo – Something given for something else.

Quorum – Number of members of a group required to be present to transact business.

RSVP – Answer an invitation. Period.

Reticent – Disposed to be silent. File under listen more than you speak.

Sagacious – Having practical sense.

Serendipity – An aptitude for making valuable discoveries by accident.

Thank you – See please.

Think – (as in, before you speak)

Uptake – Mental grasp.

Utilitarian – Concerned with usefulness, not beauty.

Validate – To substantiate. Give someone validation today.

Vanguard – The forefront in a movement.

Wag – Mischievous or witty person.

Whimsical – Given to "in the moment".

X-factor – That indefinable moment which makes "a moment".

Yadayadayada – Slang for etcetera.

Yen – A desire.

Zilch – Zero.

Zippy – Full of energy.

SPINNING LATIN

I would like to debunk the widely held belief that the study of Latin is, to quote those whiny students that seem to emerge in every generation, "Latin is a dead language." There's a glib little rhyme that's almost as old as the language itself:

> *Latin's a dead language*
> *Dead as it can be.*
> *It killed the Roman Empire,*
> *And now it's killing me.*

Can't you just picture the writer of that lyric? A lazy underachiever with a penchant for whining whose university wit goes to waste on lines like those. I'm here to suggest that, with an open mind, the study of Latin can enrich one's vocabulary treasure chest. Many French phrases, such as "bon appétit" and "je ne sais quoi", have become incorporated into our daily language. Likewise with the Spanish "mi casa es su casa." For that matter, Latin phrases, such as "status quo" and "m.o." (modus operandi) are not thought of as foreign because, you see, we are Americans. Innately at least, we feel that everything is ours for the taking, including the adoption of those select foreign phrases that seem to serve us. But, that thesis is the subject of another book. I'm suggesting that with an open mind, one can appreciate and use Latin not only to help with the study of our more difficult English grammar, but to colorize and season our everyday language.

As a language arts educator, I swear by the use of Latin in the English classroom. Its word endings, conjugations and declensions can be utilized in the study of morphology and syntax, not to mention words from Latin as vocabulary. In this book, however, I am not even speaking with my "teacher voice". Rather, I am speaking as an advocate of all resources one can use to improve vocabulary. There are several good books devoted to the subject of Latin as a vocabulary tool, but I'd like to focus on the fun, the colorful, and even offbeat, Latin phrasings that anyone can commit to memory and call upon at a cocktail reception, convention, or even at a job interview, not only to impress, but to express a thought that would require many more words in English. Here are some fun Latin phrasings that might serve the purpose:

Latin Phrase	Translation
Canis meus id comedit	My dog ate it.
Clamo, clamatis, omnes clamamus pro glace	I scream, you scream, we all scream for ice cream.
Cogito ergo sum	I think, therefore I am.
Devoro ergo sum	I drink, therefore I am.
Die dulci fruere	Have a nice day.
Fac ut gaudeam	Make my day.
Mellita, domi adsum	Honey, I'm home.
Nunc prehende uxore meam sis	Take my wife, please.
Ut si	As if
Fac ut vivas	Get a life.
Radix lecti	Couch potato
Sona si latine loquens	Honk if you speak Latin.
Rhino laborare	Nose job (loose translation)
Sit vis nobiscum	May the force be with you.

No doubt you have heard these:

Bona fide	Good faith, credentials
Carpe diem	Sieze the day.
Caveat emptor	Let the buyer beware.
Defacto	Of fact, it is.
Persona non grata	Unwelcome person.
Sine quo non	Without which, nothing.
Tempus fugit	Time flies.
Ixie dixit	He said it himself.
Verbatim	Word for word.
Habeas corpus	You have the body.

E pluribus Unum   Out of many, one.
Quid Pro quo   You scratch my back; I'll scratch yours.
Forte consulto   Accidentally on purpose (oxymoron).

THANKS TO THE BARD

There have been entire books written on the subject of words coined by William Shakespeare. I have once again chosen a one-a-week list to add to your vocabulary and realm of understanding and have verified with the *Essential High School Dictionary* published by the Princeton Review. Perhaps you've been to a Shakespeare play and been able to discern the meanings of some of these in context, or perhaps you'd like to sound more literary, more confident. I challenge you to pepper your communications with some of these, or at least be confident when you hear them that you know "from whence they came".

Sometimes, the reading of Shakespeare gets a bad rap, and many times students are turned off before they begin because they perceive his writings to be difficult, but actually, the opposite is true. "The Bard" was the writer of the common people, those who could afford the mere pittance that it may have cost to attend a production at The Globe. His sense of humor and fun with words is to be enjoyed, and a book about words would not be complete without acknowledgement of his contributions. So, enjoy some of The Bard's wordabulous words.

Auspicious – Promising success. In *The Tempest*, the magician Prospero promises "calm seas, auspicious gales" for the journey home.

Baseless – Having no foundation. From *The Tempest*.

Birthplace – Where one was born. In *Coriolanus*, the title character says, "My birthplace hate I."

Cold-blooded – Without emotion. In *King John*, Constance calls those who have betrayed her "cold-blooded".

Dauntless – Not to be intimidated. In *Henry VI*, King Louis of France advises Henry's wife, Margaret, to let her dauntless mind help her to rise above her misfortunes.

45

Dwindle – To make less. In *Henry IV*, Falstaff describes the aging process by saying that his years dwindle.

Fitful – Spasmodic. Irregular. In *Macbeth*, the title character, who has murdered King Duncan, proclaims that life has been a "fitful fever". (The Bard was also a frequent user of alliteration.)

Green-eyed – Have you ever heard the emotion of jealousy referred to as a "green-eyed monster"? Thank Shakespeare for introducing the term in *Othello*. Iago warns Othello about the power of jealousy as ". . . the green-eyed monster, which doth mock the meat it feeds on."

Hot-blooded – Excitable. Impetuous. Passionate. In *The Merry Wives of Windsor,* Falstaff appeals to the "hot-blooded" Greek gods to aid him in his amorous desires.

Ill-starred – Unlucky. Ill-fated. When Othello kills Desdemona, he refers to her as "ill-starred".

Leap-frog – A game in which players take turns leaping over one another. Even in serious plays, Shakespeare employed comic relief. Henry V regrets that he cannot win a lady at leap-frog.

Lonely – Solitary. In *Coriolanus*, the title character uses an apt simile: "I go alone like a lonely dragon."

Misgivings – Feelings of doubt. Cassius expresses mistrust toward Marc Antony by saying, "My misgiving still falls . . . to the purpose."

Negotiate – To deal or bargain. In *Much Ado About Nothing*, Claudio says, "Let every eye negotiate for itself."

Puke (puking) – Slang for vomit. In *As You Like It*, Jacques expresses his low view of human beings by saying, "At first the infant/mewling and puking in his nurse's arms. . ." This one is a personal favorite of eighth graders, when I introduce the "fun side" of Shakespeare.

Quarrelsome – Argumentative. In *Taming of the Shrew*, Petruchio's servant says, "My master's grown quarrelsome." Who wouldn't? After all, he was trying to tame a shrew.

Reclusive – Living in seclusion. In *Much Ado About Nothing*, Friar Francis says, "You may conceal her in some reclusive and religious life."

Sanctimonious – Hypocritically religious. In *Measure For Measure*, a character is called "a sanctimonious pirate".

Well-bred – Having the behavior of good breeding. In *Henry IV*, Lord Bardolph refers to an informant as "well-bred and of good name".

Zany – Whimsically comical. In *Love's Labors Lost*, the king says, "Some (women) carry tales. . . some zany."

BYOW (BRING YOUR OWN WORDS)

Strategically placed to follow the chapter on Shakespeare's coinages, I enjoy blending and creating my own words, especially when I feel that there's no word in the dictionary that adequately conveys the precise concept I'm trying to name or feeling I'm trying to express. You won't have to read too many of these to realize that this chapter is for fun. My students and I enjoy their word coinages, which we call "sniglets" in class. Even if others don't always know the meaning of the words you coin, you can explain to them. It's communication. It's connection. It's "wordabulous". Enjoy, and don't take the following too seriously.

Ambusheled – (verb) The act of having an entire nation under a spell for eight, perhaps 12 years.

Blamorama – (noun) Blame-fest that takes place after a project that fell flat.

Cardioholic – (noun) One who is addicted to aerobic exercise.

Cosmobe – (noun) Female who sips cosmopolitans, so as to look sophisticated like the characters on *Sex and The City.*

Domology – (noun) The art of taking one strand of hair and trying to stretch it over an entire bald head.

E-male – (noun) That rare boyfriend who will watch E! television network with you.

Flibbertigiblets – (noun) Those new cellulite dimples that appear after Thanksgiving.

Gingersnap – (verb) To have a breakdown after watching too many *Gilligan's Island* reruns.

Honeydue – (adverb) The time you are to be picked up for a date.

Irate – (adjective) Iran and Iraq.

Juggernought – (noun) A deficit in chest measurement.

Kibitular – (adjective) Having annoying tendencies.

Licketysplitend – (verb) Smoothing stray hair by moistening fingers.

Male chauvinist piglet – (noun) A small boy who mimics his dad's attitude toward females.

Misteright – (noun) My husband. He tells me every day.

Nickelodious – (adjective) An afternoon of babysitting with a 5-year-old child.

Popeilings – (noun) Remnants left over from chopping apples.

Proboscimony – (noun) Use of an alimony check to get a nose job.

Quackenstock – (noun) Cheap knockoff of brand of shoe popular with the prison-matron set.

Rock 'N' Rollover – (noun) State of not having to cash out a bank CD.

Sanctijudge – (noun) The philosophy of "my church is better than your church".

Serendipity Doo – (noun) Hair gel for "old hippies".

Snafufu – (noun) A gigantic mistake, but one made with such style.

Spice – (noun) Plural of spouse.

Spraycation – (noun) Using funds saved up for a trip to pressure wash the house.

Starspangular – (adjective) Badly butchered vocal performance on the national anthem.

Trackeotomy – (noun) Brain of a Nascar watcher having gone to mush.

Uppercutterage – (noun) A high school senior's put-down of a freshman.

Vocabulosity – (noun) First cousin to "wordabulous".

Wattsworld – (noun) A fantasy school in which there are no grades, no judgments, no homework, no excuses, and no grief. Only fingerpaints, nature walks, and creating stories from cloud formations.

Whinimid – (noun) A middle school student who whines about homework.

Wingnut – (noun) One who is addicted to spicy chicken.

Winocrit – (noun) A member of a religious sect who attempts to hide his glass of wine when seen at a restaurant. (see sanctijudge)

X-it – (verb) Get yourself free.

Youtubular – (adjective) "You oughtta be on television."

Zagnut – (noun) A driver on an urban freeway at rush hour.

SAY THE WORD:
THE ROLE GAMES PLAY

Word games are invaluable in developing a large, well-rounded vocabulary. Growing up as a child in the 1960s, I was enthralled by television game shows that featured words such as *Password, Pyramid* and *You Don't Say.* Crossword puzzles and games of Scrabble also filled my spare time, and as a television game show producer, I always lean toward creating games involving word-knowledge. As a teacher, I am validated each time we play word games in class. I want to share a game with you that I originally created as a dictionary search activity for my seventh grade. Cover the answers at the bottom of the page, and play along, either using the dictionary or not. If I were pitching this game to a network as a television game show, I would describe it like this: What do a hippopotamus, Cambodian leader Pol Pot, and potpourri have in common? Nothing except that each includes the word, "pot". The title of each of the following is a clue to the root word in each answer. Have fun with these. Remember that the "common root" may not always come at the beginning of the word.

Create your own "wordabulous" word games, and share them with me at Info@Wordabulous.com.

Give 'Em The Ax

1. Pay this by April 15.
2. Transmit documents by telephone.
3. Plant with blue flowers used to make linen.
4. To polish, as in a hardwood floor.
5. To become less tense.
6. Woodwind instrument played by former President Bill Clinton.
7. The earth rotates on this.
8. A character from mythology, and a brand of household cleanser.
9. The most.
10. Self-evident truth that requires no proof.

Answers:
1. Tax
2. Fax
3. Flax
4. Wax
5. Relax
6. Sax
7. Axis
8. Ajax
9. Maximum
10. Axiom

"Pot" Luck

Remember the "root" will not always be the first syllable.

1. Flagship food product of Idaho.
2. African mammal who lives in rivers.
3. White element essential to a healthy diet.
4. The side of a triangle opposite to the right angle.
5. River which flows into the Chesapeake Bay.
6. Type of old-fashioned stove named for its protruding base.
7. Thick soup made of vegetables.
8. Work of literature produced for financial gain.
9. A fragrant mixture of dried flower petals.
10. Cambodian "bad guy" leader.

Answers:
1. Potato
2. Hippopotamus
3. Potassium
4. Hypotenuse
5. Potomac
6. Pot belly
7. Pottage
8. Pot boiler
9. Potpourri
10. Pol Pot

In The Black

1. Black fruit, or a communication device.
2. Slate for writing on with chalk.
3. Payment extorted by intimidation.
4. A theoretical object in space through which no light can escape.
5. Maker of horseshoes.
6. A card game of 21.
7. Actor whose name is the "turnaround" of number six.
8. Venomous spider.
9. Pirate for whom a resort in Bermuda is named.
10. "Death personified" in a movie character portrayed by Brad Pitt.

Answers:

1. Blackberry
2. Blackboard
3. Blackmail
4. Black hole
5. Blacksmith
6. Blackjack
7. Jack Black
8. Black Widow
9. Blackbeard
10. Joe Black

Pan For Gold

1. Black and white mammal of China.
2. Sudden overwhelming fear.
3. Brand name of household cleanser, "Spic and. . .?
4. Insulin-producing organ.
5. In mythology, she opened a box of evil.
6. A strip of land, or to beg.
7. Wild uproar.
8. Candy made from almond paste.
9. "Tall and tan and young and lovely. . ." was the girl from this South American location.
10. Brand of toothpaste whose spokesman was Bucky Beaver.

Answers:
1. Panda
2. Panic
3. Span
4. Pancreas
5. Pandora
6. Panhandle
7. Pandemonium
8. Marzipan
9. Ipanema
10. Ipana

It's A Dog's Life

1. Slang for a frankfurter.
2. Elvis sang, "You ain't nothin' but a . . . what?
3. Longshot to win, and a cartoon character who was "humble and lovable".
4. Container used to take food home from a restaurant.
5. Confounded expression, "I'll be. . . what?"
6. One who is in disfavor is said to be in the what?
7. To fold paper at the corner.
8. Hottest period of the summertime.
9. System of church principles.
10. Gidget's television boyfriend.

Answers:
1. Hot Dog
2. Hound Dog
3. Underdog
4. Doggie Bag
5. Doggone
6. Dog House
7. Dog Ear
8. Dog Days
9. Dogma
10. Moondoggie

Knock On Wood

1. Borough of Los Angeles characterized by the famous hillside sign.
2. Red-headed cartoon character famous for his "ha-ha-ha-ha-ha".
3. Actor whose signature line was, "Go ahead, make my day."
4. *Peanuts'* comic strip bird, or famous outdoor rock concert of the '60s.
5. Type of musical instrument which includes a reed mouthpiece.
6. Large California tree immortalized by singer Neil Young.
7. Brand name of antique typewriter, and last name of *American Idol*, Carrie Underwood.
8. *Blondie's* comic strip husband, also a sandwich named after him.
9. Robin Hood's forest home.
10. "Scandinavian" title of song by Lennon and McCartney.

Answers:
1. Hollywood
2. Woody Woodpecker
3. Eastwood
4. Woodstock
5. Woodwind
6. Redwood
7. Underwood
8. Dagwood
9. Sherwood
10. Norwegian Wood

WORDABULOUS CLASSROOM ACTIVITIES

If you are a teacher, I hope you'll try some of these activities with your students. No, they are not just for English class. Any subject area can feature the creation of a "dictionary" of vocabulary terms. Any of the following suggestions can be adapted to any subject.

Play television game show word games. *Jeopardy, Password, Wheel of Fortune (hangman),* and *Who Wants To Be Wordabulous* can all lend themselves to vocabulary studies.

Board and classic games such as Bingo and Tic Tac Toe can also be adapted. My students love playing Bingo with their vocabulary lists. First, they each create a bingo card by writing words in squares on an oversized bingo card. These can be bought at any teacher supply store. (This only works when the vocabulary list consists of more than 25 words, so that every card that is created is not identical. If they were, then each student would yell "Bingo!" at the same time.) After they have filled in the 25 bingo squares, I take them up and check for spelling. Then (usually the next day) I redistribute the cards, and the game begins. I call out definitions, and they locate the appropriate words on their cards. The game proceeds as a regular game of bingo would.

Make a vocabulary "quilt". Use squares of construction paper and sharpie pens. Write each word pertinent to a given subject on each square, along with a summarized definition. Assemble with glue sticks and roll paper. Display "quilts" on a wall, or hang from the ceiling.

Make desk calendars. You must begin this activity around Thanksgiving because it will involve each student finding 365 words. First, they look up each word and write the definition, part of speech, and language of origin in their notebooks. "Then, on each page of a blank note pad, they each write the month, the day, and the word information." They may choose their own themes for their calendars or personalize them for their recipients of the gift calendars.

Middle schoolers like to make greeting cards and write thank-you notes. On the various holidays and special occasions throughout the year, use these as opportunities for vocabulary lessons.

On a given subject, provide a vocabulary word bank. They love to create crossword puzzles and *Word Finder* graphs.

Speaking of word banks, take a cardboard box that has a top. Cover it with roll paper and make letters that say, "word bank". Give extra points for each 3x5 card they "deposit" in the word bank. Each card should once again have the word, its part of speech, language of origin, and definition.

Never underestimate the value of an old-fashioned "bee". Whether it be a spelling, definition or question-and-answer competition, they love to have teams and "defeat the opponent".

As you create your own activities and have success stories to share, e-mail them to me at wattsd2@comcast.net.

AFTER-WORDS

As my love affair with words continues, I hope yours is just beginning. A famous song says, "The best things in life are free." I say that words fit that category. They're free for the taking . . . or for the using. Let your words work for you.

Thanks again to the Princeton Review's *Essential High School Dictionary.* Thanks to the Game Show Network and the National Vocabulary Championship. Thanks to my students over the years and all the "words" we have exchanged. Thanks to Chuck and Penney and Jennifer and Cheryl and Brad and Allen and Nelson and all my other colleagues and friends who are forced to listen to my "Lucy Ricardo" ideas.

I don't claim to be an expert at anything. When it comes to words, though, I want to play the game. Words. . . embrace them, own them, listen to them, and most of all, like your friends, choose them carefully. That's about all I have to say because after 20 years of teaching, I have acquired ADD. (It is catching, you know.) No, seriously, we are called upon to do so many varied tasks during the course of our days, that our attention span on any one activity is shortened daily.

This treatise, by most standards, would be considered a short book. In fact, for most, it can be read in one sitting. I don't claim to be wordy, just wordabulous. You can be, too. Gotta go now. After grading final exams, I'm curling up with a good dictionary.

Sources

The Essential High School Dictionary. Princeton Review. 2006.

Jay, Timothy. *Why We Curse: A Neuro-Psycho-Social Theory of Speech.*
Philadelphia, Pa. J. Benjamins Publisher. 1999.

What Others Say

When I first met award-winning artist/author/educator Debbie Watts, I was amazed by her heart-felt enthusiasm and wealth of ideas. In just a few short months, she developed her 'Word Woman' persona to creatively coach high school students for the National Vocabulary Championship. When the Game Show Network named her the National Vocabulary Championship Coach of the Year, Ms. Watts knew she had discovered her true calling – to help people improve their lives by using the right words. With her third book, 'Wordabulous!', 'Word Woman' takes readers on a power word mission for success. This wonderfully inspiring book is sure to test your knowledge, tickle your wordy-bones, and inspire you to greatness. I'm very proud to be working with America's lady of words, and also eager to see how her latest 'Word Woman' adventure unfolds in classrooms, business offices and households around the world.

– Chuck Whiting, Publicist/Composer/Author, Whiting Publicity & Promotions and Shine Time Books

———

Debbie Watts offers a delightful compendium of words, meanings, and joyous play with the English language. Whether you want to inspire students to love vocabulary or just want to savor the flavor of both new and familiar words, you'll find tons of word fun in this book.

– Candy Paull, author of *The Art of Abundance, The Art of Encouragement,* and *The Art of Simplicity.*

———

Kudos to Mrs. Watts for creating a fun and engaging character to help her students experience the power and wonder of words.

– Carla Cushman, Teacher Center Supervisor, Sumner County Schools in Gallatin, Tenn.

The power of words makes us human and should be a lifelong journey. 'Wordabulous!' is not to be read with the idea of 'finishing', but rather continuing the journey. . . and what a rich and rewarding one it will be.

– Cheryl Treadway, Faculty, National Paideia Institute

––––––––

'Word Woman' and her concept 'Wordabulous!' takes all (referring to Debbie's selection as National Vocabulary Championship Coach of the Year).

– David Nurnberg, CEGNY (Promotion Coordinator, National Vocabulary Championship, Game Show Network)

––––––––

Words are the paint we use to create the pictures of our lives. The larger our vocabulary, the more vibrant our tapestry. The concept of 'Wordabulous!' is a terrific idea.

– Lori Kissinger, Executive Director of VSA Arts Tennessee and a member of the Department of Speech and Theatre for Middle Tennessee State University

––––––––

The Saucy Sisters wholeheartedly recommend 'Wordabulous!' We love words. Always have. And we're usually pretty good at stringing a bunch of them together. But never have we laughed so hard over a discussion of words. Words, of course, are serious business. But Debbie has made their usage in everyday situations something to smile about... and to remember.

She covers little words and big words. And even four-letter words (although some of those you'll have to guess at because she left out certain letters for the sake of propriety). Our one disappointment was her chapter on BYOW. We were all set to get out the Riedel stemware until we realized she wasn't talking about wine.

Our vinous habits aside, we wholeheartedly recommend 'Wordabulous!' ... and you can quote us on this: If you want to get farther in life and in your career, you'll 'knead' this book. It will have 'duel' benefits: You'll learn 'alot' and your language will illicit very much 'prays'. So go 'by' it!

– Authors/talk show hosts Barbara Nowak & Beverly Wichman (The Saucy Sisters)

Increasing vocabulary is like gathering tools. The more tools you collect, the better.

– Christian, eighth grade language arts student

About The Author

Debbie Mathis Watts has loved words as long as she can remember. A talkative and literate child, she discovered at an early age that everything that mattered to her could be obtained or retained by the correct usage of the right words. Although she didn't always use them at the right time, she knew there was undeniable power in words.

It isn't surprising then that words ultimately played a significant role in her career. The author, educator, speaker, musical performer and television producer has dedicated her "wordabulous" career to show others how "life can be improved, enjoyed and celebrated through the knowledge and appreciation of words." Now she is stepping onto the national stage by penning the new book, *Wordabulous!: Celebrating the 'Positive Power' of Words*.

Watts is well prepared to take her message into the vocabulary stratosphere. For over a decade, she has inspired teenagers as an award-winning teacher in Hendersonville, Tenn. Before that, she was a highly respected writer and producer of game shows for Reid-Land Productions and an acclaimed performer at Opryland and other venues.

Today, she is known as "Word Woman," a "guru" of grammar, a "high priestess" of pronouns and prepositions, a "comma-mama", and among other things, a "woman of words".

"I'm an advocate for life being wordabulous," Watts says with a hearty laugh. "Word Woman fights her arch enemy, 'apathy', and inspires her students to 'arm themselves with an empowering vocabulary'. Come reach into my bag of tricks. The results will be magical."

In 2007, the Game Show Network and The Princeton Review asked Watts to coach high school students for the National Vocabulary Championship. She used her "Word Woman" persona (infectious, high-spirited personality) to motivate her students to become "word wizards". Her "Wonder Woman"-like character would appear in class in full regalia, wearing a magical headdress and wrist deflectors. Each school day, she led a percussion-accented vocabulary ritual, encouraging students to drop newly discovered words into a large box marked "word bank".

Her creative antics for student motivation were recognized in 2008 when she was named National Vocabulary Championship Coach of the Year. She won a cash prize of $1,000, another $1,000 in books for her school, and an invitation to attend the nationally televised competition in Santa Monica, Calif. The honor landed her news media exposure across Middle Tennessee. She says it was one of the happiest moments in her life and a turning point in her career.

"I was not only validated that my attention-getting behavior must have yielded some results, but that perhaps people of all ages and careers can benefit from what I call 'adventures in vocabulary'," adds the word diva with a smile. "That's when I coined the new word 'wordabulous', a concept that life can be improved, enjoyed, and, if you will, celebrated through the knowledge and appreciation of words."

Watts, who sidelines as a vocabulary consultant and staff development speaker for Tennessee public schools, is eager to share her insights with groups across the country.

The author already has inspired fellow teachers with the book, *Eat My Chalk Dust: Creative Teaching With a Sense of Humor.* Her first book, *Diary of a Nashville Lady: Recollection & Recipes,* is based on a historical/fictional character she created named Elise Bransford. Also on the "writing board" are two heartfelt stories for children.

From 1984-94, Watts gained invaluable experience as the head writer and producer on the game shows *Fandango* and the Ace Award-winning *Top Card* for Reid-Land Productions. She continues to develop free-lance projects for television and is a contributing writer for Games Magazine and Reader's Digest.

An accomplished vocalist, pianist, songwriter and actor, she began her music career at Opryland USA. She has performed regularly as a piano-vocalist at Loew's Vanderbilt Hotel since 1993. She has penned the television theme for *Play It Again, Nashville* and songs for Michael Twitty *(Debbie Don't Do Dallas)* and Bill Anderson *(Fathers and Sons and Sheet Music).*

"In today's fast-paced society, the words you use can mean the difference between success or failure," she continues in a more serious tone. "Words are low-hanging fruit – there for the taking. Why are people unwilling to pick the fruit?"

In both 2007 and 2008, Watts was named "Teacher of the Year" by the Veterans of Foreign Wars for inspiring her students in the annual "Patriot's Pen" essay contest. She earned a bachelor's degree in English and music from Lipscomb University and a master's degree in creative writing, composition and literature from Austin Peay State University in Clarksville, Tenn.

Watts and her husband, Ray, live in Hendersonville. Their daughter, Brittany, has two children.

To book Watts as a guest speaker, or for information about her vocabulary consulting business, visit **www.wordabulous.com** or write her at **info@wordabulous.com.**

Notes

Notes

Notes